Moments

One Woman's Soul-Baring Journey through Poetry

Marquita Holloman

ISBN 978-1-0980-9528-4 (paperback)
ISBN 978-1-0980-9529-1 (digital)

Christian Faith Publishing, Inc.
832 Park Avenue
Meadville, PA 16335
www.christianfaithpublishing.com

Printed in the United States of America

A Sad Christmas

(My very first poem, the writing of a naïve child before she knew Christ)

My grandfather passed away on Christmas Eve
It was sad, we cried, and we grieved.
But he's not in pain; he's at eternal rest.
Still, to me, that isn't the best.
Sometimes, I say, I say to myself,
Marquita, you know he was in very bad health.
Then, I say to myself again, I wish it was
the beginning instead of the end.

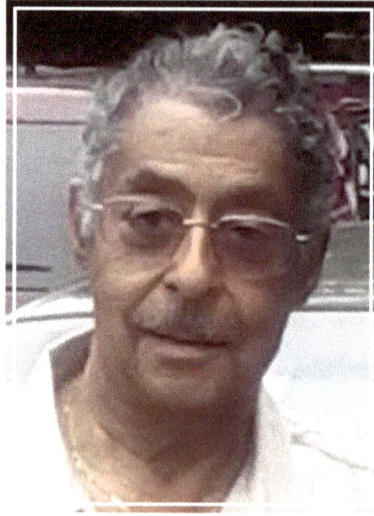

1-2-3-4

1-2-3-4 Is a meaning of life, and a life lived no more.

1-2-3-4 Is a life passed down to others, which created descendants, fathers, and mothers.

1-2-3-4 Standing alone have not a meaning, but together, Oh, Wow, have the numbers created beings.

If the numbers didn't exist, nor would she, but He, the Most High, knew what the journey would be.

The numbers were given by God, who created a being. They manifested into a life, a man worthy of living.

1—Turns into the eleventh month of the year.

2—Turns into the twenty-second, the day he would appear.

3—Nineteen thirty-three, the year God whispered life into the infant's ear.

4—So dreadful! The fourth day of the tenth month was the worst year! The day she heard the words that changed her life forever, "He's gone, my dear."

November 22, 1933, was the month, the day, the year, the time he made his way out of the womb and breathed in his first air.

He'd begin life in this world, many journeys planned. Many sunrises lived until God said, "Take My hand."

Your life here is done, but there is much more yet to see;

As I placed you in the womb, it's time to come back home to Me.

All of your questions will be answered, many mysteries revealed; no time to look back, your family will heal.

1-2-3-4 Standing alone have not a meaning, but together, shake me to my core.

1-2-3-4 A life lived by daddy; a physical life lived no more.

A Letter from Mom

(Poem for Alzheimer's Victims)

I may not remember *You* or the things you and I would do.

I may not remember *Me* or the things you and I would see.

I don't remember what we've shared; But know that I know that you've cared.

I'm here somewhere, deep inside, but my loss of memory has caused *Me* to hide.

The day will come when all will be lost. It's with my life; I will pay an extremely high cost.

Just know that I've loved you and know that I've cared.

It's not my heart that has forgotten, but it's my mind that won't allow me to keep what we've shared.

Don't lose patience, and don't be mad. Don't even get lonely or allow your heart to be sad.

Know that I'm somewhere within, deep inside. It's not my heart that won't remember; it's my mind that forces our memories to hide.

My memories have gone and may forever be lost.

It's with my life and our memories that I will pay this bitter cost.

My mind is now gone, soon this body will follow, and when this happens, in pity, don't wallow.

Because now, I am free, and all memories have followed.

Stand tall and stand strong, for I know that you've cared, and now up in heaven all our memories I've shared.

Beneath the Pain

As she pulls back the layers, she finds only tears beneath the
pain.
She longs for the sun but finds only rain, not far beneath the
pain.
Her anguish runs deep as she searches for peace beneath the
pain.
She asks God, "Why?" through the tears, she hides beneath the
pain.
She sits silently and prays as she fakes being brave beneath the
pain.
He hears her cries and the question of "Why?" beneath the
pain.
She waits patiently as she's finally set free from the hurt,
from the pain.
As the layers of anguish and sorrow pull away, she can
finally, say,
I've found sunshine where there once was rain.
I've found happiness to replace my pain.

Broken in Darkness

Broken in darkness and sadly confused,
She longs for that someone who would become
her muse.
She once knew laughter where there is now pain.
She prays for the sunlight to replace the rain.
Her sorrow runs deep,
No one could see.
Her sorrow has a name,
Her name is me.

Cry If You Must

(But Not Too Long)

As I lay in bed, a soft voice whispered my name.
That's when I knew that my time came.
I said, "I'm not ready. I need more time."
"I need to say goodbye to my family; just one more hour will be fine."
He said, "My child, you've done all that you can."
"Your work here is over, now just take my hand."
Then I felt pressure, yet I was calm. With that, it was over;
From my body, my spirit had gone.
I flew to the heavens; the sun was so warm.
I saw every face and felt the love that adorned.
It's over. I'm free. I had to move on.
So, cry if you must, but not too long.

Heaven Awaits Me

Heaven awaits me, my home beyond the sky.
God said, "Come to Me," so please, family, don't cry.
He called me by name, saying that my time has come;
My time here is over; my work here is done.
But Lord, I cried; Please, one final goodbye.
Look at how my family is hurting. Just look as they cry.
My child, he replied, the Comforter will come to ease
their pain.
He will heal their wounds until I call them by name.
"Now, come," He said. I've prepared a place just for you.
Your pain is over. Your suffering is through.
Come, receive your wings and fly.
If your family knows me, there is no final goodbye.

Her Truth

Her truth was that she hid so well
the pain that created her prison of hell.
She cried silent tears no one could see
and longed for the one who would set her free.
She dreamed of a sun that would warm her face.
Her truth was that she wanted someone to embrace,
someone to heal the wound in her soul,
someone to complete her and make her whole.
Then he came; her knight, her mate.
She never saw it coming, this twist of fate.
She then shed the skin that concealed her sorrow
and finally realized that there was a tomorrow.
She felt the long-awaited sun on her face
and the love from a strong and powerful embrace.
She knew when he held her so close and so tight
that she would never live another teary night.
Her fate was to find a love that was true.
Her truth was found when she found you.

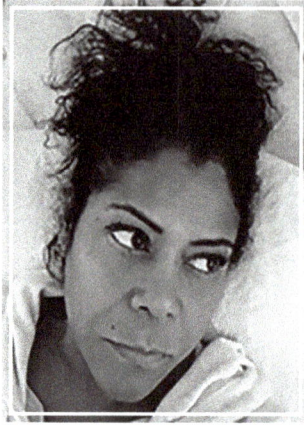

Here I Lie

My mind races. Thoughts won't
cease, so here I lie.
I think, was my choice right for
me? If so, why cry?
I can't stop thinking, so here I lie.
I am still, rigid, not wanting to be
Touched, so here I lie.
Am I living in deceit? If so, again, I
lie.
Will I ever do what's best for me
before I die?
When will I put me first?
Perhaps, I'll continue to lie until
my final goodbye.

Hey, You!

Hey, You! Just who do you think you are?
Hey, You! This time you've gone way too far!
You're the Creator of chaos; you interject yourself in our lives!
You are the Destroyer of homes who flirts with our husbands and steals our wives!
Hey, You! Yes, You! I know who you are!
You're Destruction! You're Odious! The most wicked by far!
You think that you've won because I stumbled and fell?
It will not be that easy, for I drink from God's well!
Hey, You! Yes, You! It's you, I can tell!
You're a Falsifier, a Trickster, and Coward; it's in the shadows you dwell!
Hey, You! It's, Me! Do you know who *I am?* I am God's child; He calls *me* by name!
He is the Creator, Alpha, *and* Omega, whom *I* know so well!
He said that your time here is up!
He commands you back to hell!

I Am Epitome

I've had triumphs and tragedy.
I made it through with God and my family.
I've had highs, and I've had lows.
Some felt like knockdown fights with powerful blows!
Through it all, I kept going; no, I didn't stop.
Yes, I dropped, but it was to my knees.
To God, I would pray and sometimes question, "Why me?"
There I would stay until I heard a strong yet gentle voice say;
"I chose you, my daughter, my child,
For I know that you are not filled with pride.
I know that you can take it and teach others what you learn.
I know that you will be compassionate, yet you will be stern."
So, when you see me down, no, don't pity me.
For I am Strength!
I am Confidence!
I am Love!
I Am Epitome!

It's Real

This thing is Real! It ain't no hoax!
It's been downplayed by many; some even make
jokes.
They refuse to wear masks that keep you and me safe.
Well, reality sure has of way of smacking us dead in
the face.
I am now living with pain, not knowing my outcome;
As others continue to live carelessly while having their
fun.
People are dying! Why can't they see? Why do they
refuse to take this seriously?
There is no conspiracy!
No, this isn't a hoax!
COVID-19 is real!
The experts aren't duping us, and they are not blowing
smoke!

Fly

(With the Wings God Gave You)

Fly with the wings God gave you.
Soar to the heavens knowing He saved
you.
Your time on earth was arduous and
long;
Now, all of your weaknesses God has
made strong.
Soar, with the wings God gave you.
You are now forever strong because
He saved you.

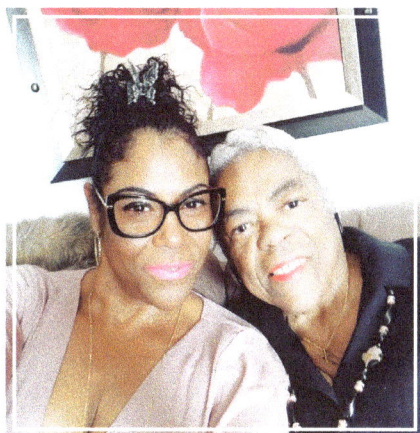

Mommy

Mom, you're always there to share a
shoulder or an ear. Even your stern
words are ignited by care.
You've been through a great deal and
suffered much loss. Although you
emerged Victorious, a piece of your heart
was the cost.
When I look at you, I see a strong
matriarch who leads with understanding;
who taught us to always support one
another even when it's overwhelming and
demanding.
Through these eyes, I see a woman,

independent and strong; who has no
problem telling us when we are wrong.
A mother is what everyone else may see;
but as your baby, although grown, you'll
always be "Mommy" to me.

My Sister, My Friend

First, we were sisters who became friends;
A bond God created and blessed with His
hands.
A bond that's been tested but will never die.
A bond that created my greatest ally.
You're always around to share a laugh or a
shoulder when I cry;
You do it without judgment, not even a
castigating sigh.
Yes, first we were sisters, now you're forever, my
friend;
A friendship that will continue to be tested,
and yet, will never end.

Retrospection, Introspection, Reflection

Retrospection, Introspection, Reflection. What does it all mean?
You look inside you? I look inside me?
We then ask ourselves, "At this point in life, am I where I want to be?"
No time for self-pity. No time for regret.
Just see the change you want to be and stop looking back.
Move forward! Trudge on!
Continue to look up, and if you feel lost from your God, ask for help.
Retrospection, Introspection, Reflection. What does it mean to me?
Looking in the mirror, at these brown eyes, and asking, "What do I see?"
I see someone who knows pain, heartbreak, and misery.
But looking into the soul of this woman of God, the greatest thing I see is not her struggle, but her faith and her VICTORY!
Retrospection, Introspection, Reflection. What does it all mean?
Rhetorically, I ask you, should God intervene?

Sisters

Although there are times when we
disagree,
We are sisters now, and sisters we will
forever be.
Our bond is steadfast, our sisterhood
strong.
We share a love that will withstand any
wrong.
Sisters we are and will forever be,
Sisters for life, you and me.

Strength

Strength manifests itself in many ways.
It's mental, physical, emotional, and it never strays.
At times, we may have to dig deep to find it;
But when we do, it gives us power over the adversary;
and our fears, Strength binds it.
It's what makes us move forward and press on.
It's what God gave us the day we were born.
Believe it or not, Strength is always there.
When we don't see it in ourselves, it's seen by those
who care.
So, when you think all is lost, and there's nothing
more;
Reach for *your* Strength, and with God, you will soar!

The Mistakes I've Made

(A Note to My Children)

The mistakes I've made were many, not few.
But I've lived, and I've learned as I was
supposed to do.
I've loved, and I've lost. I've hurt, and I've cried.
Some of those I've hurt remain by my
side. Some are gone, moved on, or died.
But the two of you are special, truly a gift
from God; my heart, my soul, my love
and my pride.
A love so strong. A bond so tight. For you
I'd give my very last breath, my life in a fight.
Yes, the mistakes I've made were many, not few.
Two mistakes never made were the two of you.

The Monkey

Why did you do it? You knew of the struggle.
That monkey you couldn't shake, but with
him, you continued to huddle.
I saw the pain in your eyes as you tried to fight
back.
But that monkey had you under constant
attack.
I know that you loved us and didn't want to go.
But running the race with that monkey, you
were just too slow.
He was always on you, riding your back.
Unfortunately, in the end, it was strength that
you lacked.
But now you are free! Now you are strong!
That Monkey is dead! That Monkey is gone!
It's your fight, I'll remember, but as I look to the
sky,
I can't help but think you did not have to die.

The Skin She's In

The skin she's in so mocha and smooth,
Hid the pain of a broken heart and a soul badly bruised.
It also masked the silent tears she cried;
The skin she's in was where she would hide.
The torment she felt was hidden so well;
no one ever knew her private
hell.
Defeated and broken until she heard a voice say,
"My child, I am here; get on your knees, and pray."
You see, I never left, and I heard all your cries.
Now the skin you're in, you no longer have to hide.
So, take my hand and hold on tight,
For I'll never leave you in the darkness of night.
The skin she's in, yes, mocha and smooth—
Is no longer broken, defeated, or bruised.
It's now filled with hope, laughter, and love
Because she believed in His word and took the hand from above.
Yes, the skin she's in, she no longer hides
Because she knows that He will be forever by her side.

To You

(A Poem for Harlan)

To you, the one I long to meet;
Conceived out of a love so strong, so sweet.
I promise to be there each and every day.
In darkness, I'll shine a light, in case you lose your
way.
To you, I give my heart, my love;
and will encourage you to seek guidance and wisdom
from our Lord above.
I'll wipe your tears in times of sorrow and hold you
close as if there were no tomorrow.
I'll bask in your joy, triumphs, and victories.
As you can count on your parents, you can also count
on me.
My love will be unconditional, everlasting, and true.
These things, my dear Harlan, I promise to you.

Together

We knew in the beginning that this day would come,
No matter how hard we wanted to ignore it or tried to play dumb.
That day finally came as you lay on the floor and I realized by my side would you walk no more.
We promised to take the bitter with the sweet.
That taste is so sour, it's the taste of defeat.
"Give up, move on!" is what the devil would say. "Go! Leave him! Live your life your own way!"
Then I look at the clouds, the sky so bright, and remember when I needed it, you were my light.
So, together we'll go on, push through this, our plight. Together we'll go on and continue this fight.

Why Are You Killing Us?

(Is the question I ask)

Why are you killing us? Is the question I ask.
Are we doomed to continue to repeat the past?
Our ancestors fought the same fight, shed their blood, and died.
They, too, are looking down and probably asking, "Why?"
Was their battle, their struggle all done in vain?
With silent tears, I feel their pain.
Through *their* eyes, I see the blood in the street;
Blood of our sisters, our brothers, our sons, that remains under our feet.
I hear the cries of each and every one;
I see the tears that won't dry with the rising of the sun.
The struggle is arduous, it's painful, it's real, but it shouldn't have to be.
Do we live in two-thousand-twenty?
Or, have we regressed to nineteen-sixty-three?
As a people, we will continue this battle with pride in our eyes.
We will win this fight and end the cries.
Then, we, the ancestors who have ascended to heaven; our final home beyond the sky;
Will no longer have to ask, "Why are you killing us?"
Simply, just why?

Today Is Not Promised

I awoke with the sun and began my day.
Then death knocked at the door and said he
may stay.
He first took my father.
My nephew was next.
He took my brothers, which left me a mess.
He said, Today is a present.
Tomorrow, a gift.
I will come again; I will be quick, and I will be
swift.
For I lurk in the shadows to your dismay.
And the one thing I will not promise is Today.

This Black Girl

This black girl, her skin so dark and so smooth sits by the window
and reflects on her truth.

She could not remember a time when she was hosed down, bitten by
dogs, or beaten and bruised.

This black girl could not remember having to go around the back or
not being able to drink from a fountain that others had used.

This black girl gave thanks to God because she did not live the life
that was her ancestors' path.

This black girl who is now a woman looks out at the street at the
aftermath.

She is remembering a time, not long ago when her brothers and sis-
ters walked hand in hand and arm in arm yelling "Stop the
Violence!" and "End the Harm!"

This black woman her skin so dark and so smooth has tears in her
eyes as she continues to cry because her ancestors' path is now
her truth.

About the Author

Marquita Holloman is the author of *Moments, One Woman's Soul-Baring Journey through Poetry*. Marquita was raised in Montgomery County, Pennsylvania. She is a graduate from Lincoln University with a master's degree in human services and is a practicing licensed behavioral specialist. Marquita considers her faith and family to be most important to her. If she is not spending time with her mother, she is hanging out with her sisters, children, and grandson. "Writing has always been therapeutic. Anyone can journal, and everyone has at least one book in them".

CPSIA information can be obtained
at www.ICGtesting.com
Printed in the USA
BVHW060912221121
622229BV00019B/783

9 781098 095284